LYDIA
and the letters

Shoo Rayner

Oxford University Press

Oxford University Press, Walton Street, Oxford, OX2 6DP

Oxford New York Toronto
Delhi Bombay Calcutta Madras Karachi
Petaling Jaya Singapore Hong Kong Tokyo
Nairobi Dar es Salaam Cape Town

and associated companies in
Berlin Ibadan

Oxford is a trade mark of Oxford University Press

© Shoo Rayner 1987
First published 1987
Reprinted 1987, 1989, 1991
Printed in Hong Kong

ISBN 0 19 916173 9

The Lydia books are:

Lydia and her garden
Lydia and the letters
Lydia and the present
Lydia and her cat
Lydia at the shops
Lydia and the ducks

Lydia book pack: ISBN 0 19 916171 2

'Oh good,' said Lydia, 'letters.'

Lydia posted the letters in a box.

Then she emptied them out again.

She posted them high up in a drawer.

She posted them low down under the carpet.

She played postman all morning...

. . . until it was time for lunch.

'Where are my letters?' asked Mum.

Lydia couldn't remember.

Lydia looked under the carpet.

Mum looked in the drawer.

They looked everywhere until tea-time.

'Never mind', said Lydia's mum.
'I'll make some tea and toast.'

'Hooray!'